ALTERNATOR BOOKS™

SPACE IN ACTION

space STATIONS IN ACTION

An AUGMENTED REALITY Experience

Rebecca E. Hirsch

Lerner Publications ◆ Minneapolis

EXPLORE SPACE IN BRAND-NEW WAYS WITH AUGMENTED REALITY!

1. Ask a parent or guardian for permission to download the free Lerner AR app on your digital device by going to the App Store or Google Play.

2. As you read, look for this icon throughout the book. It means there is an augmented reality experience on that page!

3. Use the Lerner AR app to scan the picture near the icon.

4. Watch space come alive with augmented reality!

CONTENTS

INTRODUCTION

a YEAR IN SPACE

Astronaut Scott Kelly was heading home. In 2016 Kelly ended a 340-day mission aboard the International Space Station (ISS), a giant spacecraft that **orbits** Earth. It was the longest space mission ever for a US astronaut.

Kelly launched to the ISS on March 27, 2015. He's shown here aboard the space station on March 28.

Kelly rests after returning to Earth in 2016. It took him several weeks to get used to the planet's gravity after spending nearly a year in space.

Kelly and two Russian astronauts boarded a **capsule**. A few hours later, they were speeding back to Earth. During his time in space, Kelly orbited our planet 5,440 times and traveled more than 100 million miles (161 million km). Without the pull of gravity that we experience on Earth, the spaces between the bones in Kelly's spine expanded. When he returned to Earth, he was 2 inches (5.1 cm) taller than he was when he left.

CHAPTER 1

HISTORY OF SPACE STATIONS

In 1971 the Soviet Union, a former group of fifteen republics including Russia, launched Salyut 1, the first space station. The United States launched its first space station, Skylab, two years later. Skylab stayed in orbit for six years and was home to nine astronauts who lived on the station in three separate shifts. Another Soviet space station, Mir, was inhabited for twelve years, from 1987 to 1999.

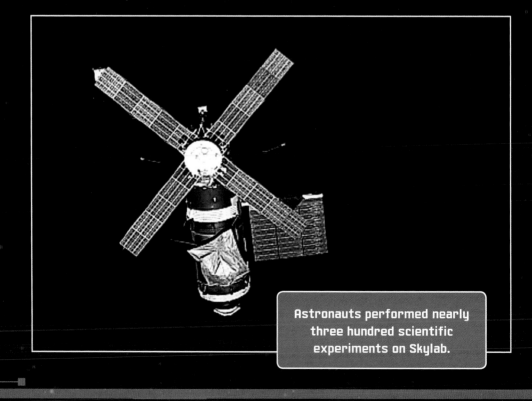

Astronauts performed nearly three hundred scientific experiments on Skylab.

Mir orbited Earth until 2001, when the Russian space agency caused the station to crash into the Pacific Ocean.

After Mir, more than a dozen countries, including Russia and the United States, worked together to build a new space station. The ISS would be bigger than Mir. Scientists would use it to study the long-term effects of weightlessness on the body and do experiments that can't be performed on Earth, such as testing equipment in zero gravity.

BUILDING THE ISS

Sections of the ISS, called **modules**, were launched separately
into orbit. The first module launched in 1998 aboard a Russian
rocket. About two weeks later, the US space shuttle *Endeavour*
brought another piece of the station to space. The crew of the
shuttle connected the two modules in orbit.

This Russian rocket
carried the Zarya Module
to space in 1998. Zarya
was the first section of
the ISS to reach orbit.

This image shows portions of five different ISS modules connected in orbit.

Over the next two years, more modules were added until the ISS was ready to house astronauts. The first space station crew arrived in 2000. People have occupied the ISS ever since.

Astronaut Peggy Whitson works in Harmony, a module that was connected to the ISS in 2007.

HOME IN SPACE

Some modules provide living spaces for crew members, while others are laboratory modules for conducting scientific research. Modules called nodes connect the parts of the space station. The ISS has air locks that astronauts use for **space walks** and ports where spacecraft that travel to the station can dock.

The ISS is as long as a football field, including the end zones. The inside of the station is about as roomy as a five-bedroom house. It has six sleeping quarters, two bathrooms, and a gym.

After launching from Earth, it takes a spacecraft about six hours to reach the ISS in orbit.

The ISS zips around the planet at about 17,500 miles (28,160 km) per hour. At that speed, it circles Earth every ninety minutes. So astronauts on the station can see sixteen sunrises every day.

The station's extreme speed allows it to stay in orbit. The high speed balances the tug of Earth's gravity, putting the station in a constant state of weightlessness. Everything and everyone on board the station floats.

CHAPTER 2

SPACE STATION BASICS

Imagine going into your home and staying there for months. No going outside! That's what most astronauts do when they travel to the ISS. Crew members live and work on the station for weeks or months at a time. Space walks are dangerous, so going outside the station is rare.

Astronaut Alexander Gerst watches a World Cup soccer match from the ISS in 2018.

ISS crew members welcome Russian astronaut Alexey Ovchinin (*background*) to the station. Ovchinin flew to the ISS in March 2019 with fellow astronauts Christina Koch and Nick Hague (*not pictured*).

Astronauts ride to the space station in a capsule launched from Earth with a rocket. In space the capsule separates from the rocket and carries the astronauts to the station. When they're ready to head home, they board a capsule and fly it back to Earth. Once the capsule reaches Earth's atmosphere, it deploys a parachute to slow its descent. The capsule lands on the ground, using tiny rockets to soften the landing.

HOW SPACE STATIONS WORK

The ISS must provide everything people need to survive. It must have drinkable water. It must have breathable air and the right temperature and humidity. It also has to communicate with Earth. Mission control centers in Houston, Texas, and Moscow, Russia, constantly monitor the station.

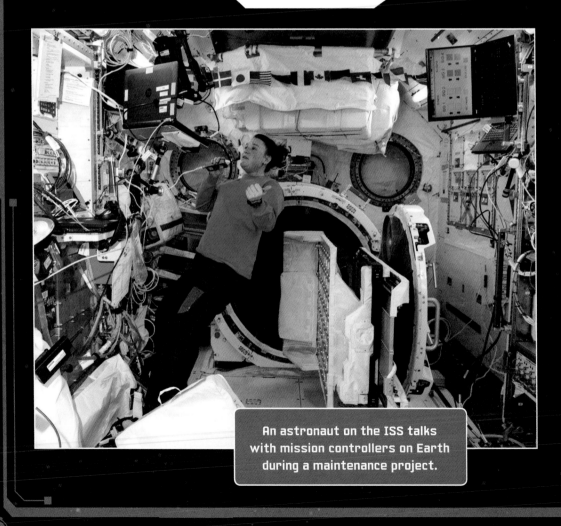

An astronaut on the ISS talks with mission controllers on Earth during a maintenance project.

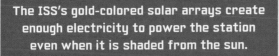

The ISS's gold-colored solar arrays create enough electricity to power the station even when it is shaded from the sun.

The station needs power to run its communications and life-support systems. **Solar arrays** on the outside of the station collect energy from the sun and convert it to electrical power. The electricity runs **radiators** that control the air temperature inside the ISS.

WATER AND AIR IN SPACE

Spacecraft carry water to the space station, but it is expensive to bring fresh water from Earth. That's why all water on the ISS is recycled. A system collects water from bathing, urine, and the sweat that **evaporates** off astronauts' bodies. The system turns the water into ultrapure drinking water. It might sound disgusting, but the recycled water is cleaner than most tap water on Earth.

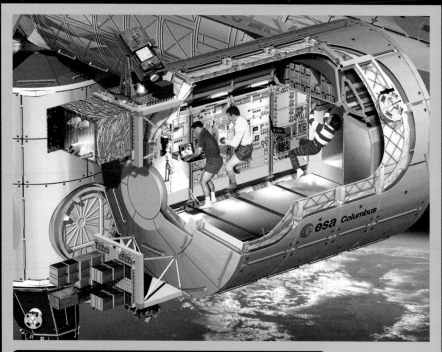

Hundreds of people from eighteen different countries have lived and worked on the ISS.

Astronauts on the ISS pose with Elektron oxygen generators, machines that create oxygen using electricity and water.

Most of the oxygen astronauts breathe on the ISS is made from water. Water is composed of hydrogen and oxygen. On the station, a machine runs a current of electricity through water, creating bubbles of hydrogen and oxygen gas that it then collects. Backup oxygen tanks are mounted on the outside of the station.

LIFE ON a SPACE STATION

CHAPTER 3

ou wake up on board the ISS. Just as at home, you must use the bathroom, wash up, and brush your teeth. How do you do those things without gravity?

The first stop is the space station bathroom. A special toilet has a personal attachment that connects to an astronaut's body and hooks onto the toilet with a hose. The toilet's gentle suction pulls waste away from the body.

Some astronauts enjoy coffee or tea when they wake up. Astronaut Samantha Cristoforetti sips a hot drink from a pouch to keep the liquid from floating away.

Astronaut Karen Nyberg squirts warm water into her hair before applying no-rinse soap.

Astronauts can't take baths or showers on the ISS. In space, water doesn't fall in a shower or stay in a tub—it floats in a blob. To keep clean, astronauts squirt a little water and no-rinse soap onto a washcloth or their hands and then rub the soap onto their skin and hair. They use toothbrushes and toothpaste, but there's no sink to spit in, so they spit into a small towel.

Most space food is **dehydrated** and stored in pouches. Astronauts squirt a little water into pouches, and the food is ready to eat. Some space food is just like food on Earth, such as nuts and pudding cups.

Astronauts make pizza in the ISS's kitchen. The space station has sleeping quarters, bathrooms, and labs for scientific research.

Astronaut Sunita Williams works out on the space station's exercise bike.

In space, astronauts must exercise more than they do on Earth. Bones and muscles have less work to do without the pull of gravity. Over time, muscles shrink and bones get less dense and can break more easily. Astronauts work out about two hours a day to keep their bones and muscles healthy. They use special exercise machines with stretchy bands to provide resistance. An exercise bicycle and treadmill use harnesses and bungee cords to hold astronauts to the machines.

CHAPTER 4

WORKING IN SPACE

How do you handle emergency repairs on the outside of a space station that's in orbit 250 miles (402 km) above Earth? With a space walk.

In 2018 two spacewalkers left the ISS to examine a spacecraft docked to the station. The vehicle had a hole no bigger than a pencil eraser. But even small holes can cause problems in space. During the space walk, the astronauts studied the damage before returning to the station.

The 2018 space walk to examine the damaged spacecraft lasted almost eight hours.

Canadarm2 attaches to a supply capsule below the ISS.

Astronauts rarely go on space walks, but sometimes they must repair the station or do other jobs outside. When they do, the robotic arm Canadarm2 might assist them. Astronauts can attach themselves to Canadarm2 and ride it to different parts of the ISS. Canadarm2 also has a hand that can grab spacecraft and bring them to the station.

Astronauts spend much of their time in space working. They maintain the station and do repairs with tools such as the Multi-Purpose Precision Maintenance Tool. It has wrenches of different sizes, a ruler, a pry bar, and instruments for measuring the thickness of wires.

Multi-Purpose Precision
Maintenance Tool

In 2014 high school senior Robert Hillan of Enterprise, Alabama, designed the Multi-Purpose Precision Maintenance Tool as part of the Future Engineers Space Tool design competition.

Wheat grows in the ISS's Advanced Plant Habitat. The door of the habitat has been removed to view the plants inside.

Astronauts also run many experiments on the ISS, including projects that will help people travel deeper into space. In 2014 astronauts began to grow a garden on the station. Future astronauts may have to grow their own food during long missions to Mars and other distant places in space.

INTO THE FUTURE

Astronauts, scientists, and engineers continue to create new ways to travel and live in space. NASA is testing the Orion capsule. It will bring people to the ISS and maybe even Mars. The Space Launch System, a new, powerful rocket, will launch the capsule into space.

NASA plans to fly an Orion capsule around the moon in 2020.

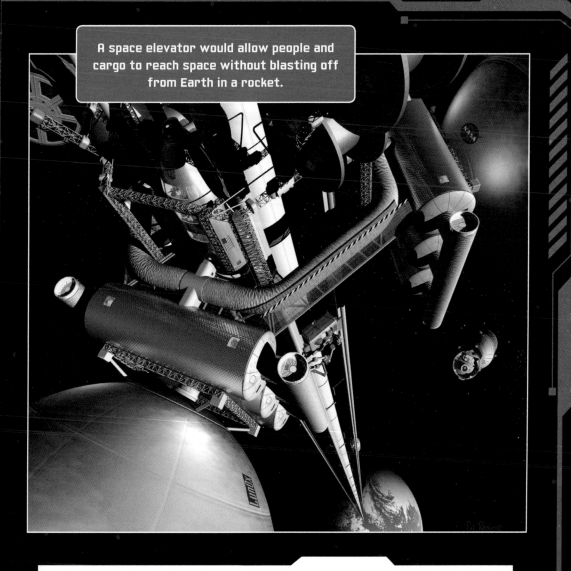

A space elevator would allow people and cargo to reach space without blasting off from Earth in a rocket.

Someday, people may ride to a future space station on a high-tech elevator. A long cable would attach the station to Earth, and a car would travel along the cable to the station. Space stations of the future will be bigger and easier to reach, allowing more people to live, work, and explore in space.

Follow the URLs below to download 3D printer files for some of the tools and vehicles in this book:

Multi-Purpose Precision Maintenance Tool, http://qrs.lernerbooks.com/MPMT

Orion, http://qrs.lernerbooks.com/Orion

Space Launch System, http://qrs.lernerbooks.com/SLS

GLOSSARY

capsule: a small spacecraft that carries astronauts to space and back to Earth

dehydrated: to have the water removed from

evaporates: changes into vapor from a liquid state

modules: independent parts of a space station

orbits: moves around a body in space

radiators: devices that transfer heat to an area

solar arrays: groups of panels made of solar cells that convert sunlight into electricity

space walks: missions that require an astronaut to move in space outside of a spacecraft or space station

FURTHER INFORMATION

Eating in Space
https://www.nasa.gov/audience/foreducators/stem-on-station
/ditl_eating

Goldstein, Margaret J. *Private Space Travel: A Space Discovery Guide.*
Minneapolis: Lerner Publications, 2017.

Kelly, Scott. *Endurance: My Year in Space and How I Got There.* New
York: Crown Books, 2018.

Kenney, Karen Latchana. *Cutting-Edge Astronaut Training.*
Minneapolis: Lerner Publications, 2020.

Larson, Kirsten. *International Space Station.* Vero Beach, FL: Rourke,
2017.

NASA: What Is a Spacewalk?
https://www.nasa.gov/audience/forstudents/k-4/stories/nasa
-knows/what-is-a-spacewalk-k4.html

NASA: What Is the International Space Station?
https://www.nasa.gov/audience/forstudents/5-8/features/nasa
-knows/what-is-the-iss-58.html

NASA Science: Water on the Space Station
https://science.nasa.gov/science-news/science-at-nasa/2000
/ast02nov_1/

Photo Acknowledgments

Image credits: Freer/Shutterstock.com, p. 2 (bottom); NASA, pp. 4, 6, 7, 10, 13, 14, 15, 17, 19, 20, 21, 22, 23, 24; NASA/Bill Ingalls, p. 5; Sovfoto/UIG/Getty Images, p. 8; ESA, p. 9; NASA/Roscosmos, p. 11; NASA/ESA, pp. 12, 18, 28; ESA/D. Ducros, p. 16; Lockheed Martin Corporation, p. 26; NASA/Pat Rawlings, p. 27. Design elements: Jetrel/Shutterstock.com; Nanashiro/Shutterstock.com; phiseksit/Shutterstock .com; MSSA/Shutterstock.com; Pakpoom Makpan/Shutterstock.com; pixelparticle/ Shutterstock.com; wacomka/Shutterstock.com; fluidworkshop/Shutterstock.com.

Cover: Ward/Shutterstock.com.

Lerner Publications Company
An imprint of Lerner Publishing Group, Inc.
241 First Avenue North
Minneapolis, MN 55401 USA

For reading levels and more information, look up this title at www.lernerbooks.com.

Main body text set in Aptifer Sans LT Pro.
Typeface provided by Linotype AG.

Library of Congress Cataloging-in-Publication Data

Names: Hirsch, Rebecca E., author.
Title: Space stations in action : an augmented reality experience / Rebecca E. Hirsch.
Description: Minneapolis : Lerner Publications, [2020]. | Series: Space in action |
    Series: Space exploration (Alternator books) | Audience: Ages 8–12. | Audience:
    Grades 4 to 6. | Includes bibliographical references and index.
Identifiers: LCCN 2019013120 (print) | LCCN 2019013929 (ebook) |
    ISBN 9781541583511 (eb pdf) | ISBN 9781541578838 (lb : alk. paper)
Subjects: LCSH: Space stations—Juvenile literature. | Space environment—Juvenile
    literature. | Life support systems (Space environment)—Juvenile literature. |
    Outer space—Exploration—Juvenile literature.
Classification: LCC TL797.15 (ebook) | LCC TL797.15 .H57 2020 (print) |
    DDC 629.44/2—dc23

LC record available at https://lccn.loc.gov/2019013120

Manufactured in the United States of America
1-46986-47855-8/13/2019